The Prestig

Lincoln:

John Banks

Photography by G H F Atkins

ISBN 1 898432 20 1

A Note about Illustrations: Lincolnshire Road Car Company Limited vehicles were renumbered in 1953 and some variation had been evident before that. The convention in this book is to **embolden** the identity of the vehicle at the time the photograph was taken.

Front Cover Illustration -- Like many another operator, Lincolnshire made use of the "dual-purpose" idea for vehicles with less austere seating within a service-bus shell. 1958's fleet number **3017** (**SFU844**) was a Bristol LS5G equipped with 41 high-backed seats in its Eastern Coach Works body. It was at Huntingdon Street, Nottingham in April 1963.

Title Page Illustration -- As befitted a Tilling fleet, Lincolnshire made much use of the Bristol Lodekka. It was perhaps less usual that the Company felt able to specify the Gardner 5LW engine for some of its Lodekkas. Increased fuel economy over a mostly flat operating terrain was the reason behind this, though it was by no means generally accepted that a small engine working hard in a big vehicle was more economical. In any case the rolling Lincoolnshire Wolds provide some distinctly hilly terrain, especially on the western escarpment edge, and not least in the city of Lincoln itself. **2365** (**NFE928**) was a 1959 LD5G. The photograph was taken at Drummond Road, Skegness in August of that year.

>> Opposite page -- Nearly a quarter of a century earlier, in July 1936, at Drummond Road, Leyland-bodied Leyland Tiger **LT409** (**FW6870**) was well-placed for a typically fine Geoffrey Atkins portrait. LT409 was a TS7 with 34-seat bodywork which had been new the previous May.

Rear Cover Illustration -- Lodekka **2372** (**NFE935**) at Huntingdon Street, Nottingham in August 1963 waiting to depart for Grantham.

Produced for the Publishers
Venture Publications, Glossop, Derbyshire
by John Banks, Romiley, Cheshire
using computerised origination

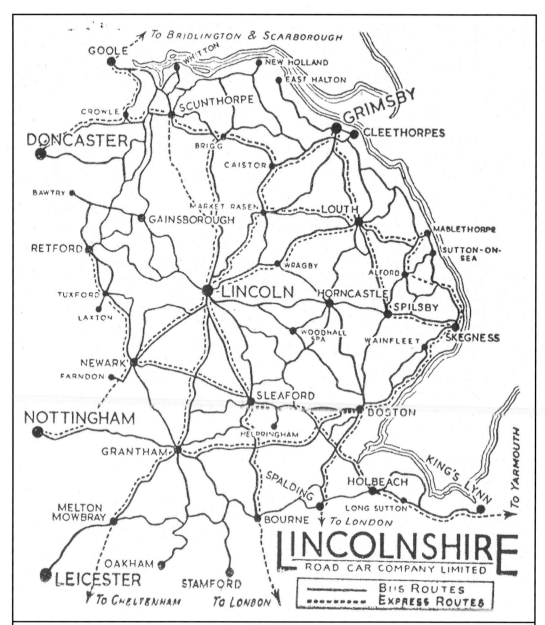

Above: *The Lincolnshire Road Car Company Limited operating area at around the change of the decade from the nineteen-fifties to the 'sixties. From Goole in the North to Leicester in the south, from Skegness on the east coast westward to Nottingham and Doncaster was a neat, compact geographical entity, although services ran into all five neighbouring counties (Yorkshire, Nottinghamshire, Leicestershire, Rutland and Norfolk). Lincolnshire's express services at this period served Bridlington and Scarborough, Great Yarmouth, Cheltenham and London. The historical link with United Automobile Services Limited survived in the services centred on Boston and Holbeach.*

Left: *In June 1958 at Huntingdon Street, Nottingham, 2077 (CVF883) was one of the oldest Bristols in the fleet and 2212 (MFU406) among the newest. 2077 was second-hand from Eastern Counties in 1954; 2212 was new in 1955.*

THE PHOTOGRAPHER

Geoffrey Atkins, well into his eighties and having taken transport photographs in nine consecutive decades, from 1927 to the present day, still occasionally takes a camera with him on walks in his hometown of Nottingham. He was first and foremost a railway photographer, in which arcane art he sought advice and tuition from some of the great names active as the decade of the nineteen-twenties turned into the 'thirties. The techniques thus begun and developed undoubtedly influenced Geoffrey Atkins's better known bus photography.

Geoffrey Atkins has never lived anywhere other than in Nottingham, the town of his birth. Lincoln, Grantham and Newark are not far away and have been frequently visited, cameras at the ready; Skegness was regularly visited for family holidays in the pre-war period: visits that produced a magnificent series of LRCC photographs. Geoffrey Atkins has his own specific aim when photographing buses and coaches, as, indeed, do most transport photographers. In his case the aim is quality rather than quantity and his material is largely devoted to forming a visual record of coachwork - Geoffrey's principal interest - on public service vehicles.

In earlier decades, when there was a clear and firm separation of municipal, company and independent operators, each able to call upon the services of any one of a long list of coachbuilders now no more, bus fleets in Great Britain had sharply defined individual character, a situation which lasted more or less to the end of 1968 and the coming of the National Bus Company. Municipality, BET, Tilling, large independent, small independent all had their favourite coachbuilder. Occasionally the unthinkable happened and an allegiance was changed. Some operators ordered from more than one provider of bodywork as a matter of policy ("dual-sourcing" in today's marketing-speak, "not putting all your eggs in one basket" in the homelier idiom of the era). Often, a skilled salesman from the opposition succeeded in "getting his product in". So although there was much variety, it was contained within what was for decades recognisably a stable environment.

Geoffrey Atkins was not a registration-number collector. The eternal search for a picture of every vehicle ever operated by his favoured companies was not for him. The Atkins technique was to produce an image of the coachbuilder's art. If only one angle was recorded, one can be sure that it shows the product to best advantage. The vehicle recorded might have been unique or one of a large batch, but if the record produced was what was wanted, it might well remain the only one. Often though, Geoffrey took a second and/or subsequent picture of a particular type.

This might not please the seeker after multiple shots of similar vehicles in traffic scenes, in different locations and on different routes. Nor, perhaps, does Geoffrey Atkins's comparative lack of interest in the smaller independents always strike a sympathetic chord in others. This is particularly noticeable in the county of Lincolnshire, always renowned for independents of whom Appleby's, Delaine, Fowler's, Grayscroft, Hornsby's, Kime's and Reliance of Great Gonerby are perhaps the most prominent. That lack of interest extended to vehicles taken over from small operators, for such vehicles have undoubtedly received less attention than the standard types supplied to the larger operators. The present writer, for example, knowing that Geoffrey had frequently been in London in the nineteen-thirties, queried the absence of TD-class Leyland Titans among Geoffrey's fine collection of pre-war London Passenger Transport Board photographs. He explained that he had seen such vehicles but that they did not interest him as much as the standard

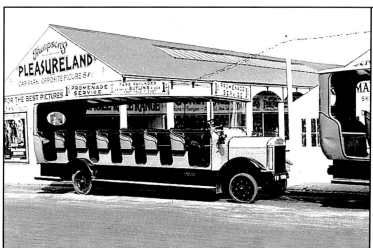

Left: A fascinating Lincolnshire precursor, Tom Carey Limited, of Skegness, ran this Vulcan runabout in a grey livery to convey trippers along the Promenade for one (old) penny. Skegness Motor Service Limited had some similar vehicles, in red livery, and acquired Carey's fleet in the early 1930s. The Vulcans passed to Lincolnshire with the Skegness Motor Service business in 1934, underwent much rebuilding and were very long-lived in the resort.

Chiswick-built types which were more representative of the LPTB as a bodywork constructor.

Geoffrey Atkins has never been profligate in his use of film. Were he the kind of photographer who rushes around bus stations and garage premises trying to pot everything in sight, paying scant regard to lighting and other conditions, he could not have produced such a remarkable, carefully compiled pictorial catalogue of coachwork development over a span of sixty years from many of the country's most interesting operators. It does not do to complain about the gaps: there are plenty of vast collections of average, not to say indifferent, quality but no other like that of Geoffrey Atkins.

Each view has been carefully chosen to be exactly what was wanted. Geoffrey has not been a fair-weather photographer, to be put off by thunderstorms, snow, or even fog: all three can be found among his masterpieces. Despite his priority, he occasionally turned his lens on to a traffic scene, or a general view in a bus station, perhaps to point up a contrast between the coachwork on adjacent vehicles. Night scenes were a speciality, too. Not many of them, it is true, but each one a masterpiece. Geoffrey's equipment - cameras, lenses and enlargers - has invariably been carefully chosen to do the job he required of it. Good equipment does not make a good photographer, but a good photographer can often be let down by inadequate tools. Not so here. Each piece of equipment, each exposure, each print from the enlarger, is designed to produce exactly the required result. And with a remarkably consistent success rate. It has not often happened that a print I would have liked to include produced Geoffrey's gentle but firm, "I would rather you didn't use that one, I wasn't happy with it".

Geoffrey's pictures were not taken with publication in mind and many never have been published. This album cannot contain all of the GHFA Lincolnshire collection. As with the volumes on East Midland and East Yorkshire, the emphasis has naturally fallen on what might be termed "the golden years". The pre-war material forms the splendid core, but the coverage extends to the first generation of rear-engined double-deckers and ends with Lincolnshire celebrating its 60th anniversary. The vehicles have been presented in chassis-make groupings: from AEC to Vulcan, followed by Leyland and Bristol as the pre-war and post-war standards.

One of the most pleasant aspects of the work on this series of albums has been choosing and discussing the photographs. Geoffrey Atkins makes me welcome from the moment he opens the door of his home to my ring on the doorbell. The kettle goes on, tea is served, and we begin the unenviable task of deciding what to leave out. Geoffrey's comments on the technical aspects of each photograph, his encyclopaedic memory about when and where each one was taken, even to the time of day, and his formidable knowledge of coachwork enliven all our discussions. As always, my grateful thanks to Geoffrey for his patience and kindness.

Once more I must acknowledge with gratitude the willing and expert help I have received from Philip Battersby, John D Watson and Ron Maybray: each in his own way has contributed much to the textual aspect of the book which would have been the poorer without them. If, in spite of their guidance, mistakes have crept in, the responsibility is mine alone.

THE COMPANY

The Lincolnshire Road Car Company Limited was mysterious and, because of that mystery, glamorous. From the writer's boyhood base in Kingston-upon-Hull, he knew that LRCC (or "Road Car" as it was universally known) buses plied their trade only a handful of miles or so away. But that short distance included the River Humber and a ferry journey. From the Pier in Hull one boarded a steam-powered vessel and was conveyed to New Holland on "the other side". (The ferries have gone now, of course. The Humber bridge has a lot to answer for...) Some people, to at least one small boy's amazement, lived on the Lincolnshire side and commuted daily via the ferry to jobs in Hull. For him, though, a river-crossing was a rare treat. There were no relations over there, but the occasional school trip to Lincoln cathedral or family outing to Mablethorpe or Skegness was an occasion to be enthused over weeks in advance and savoured for weeks after, though in neither case for reasons school or parent might have wished.

The very name of that riverside destination across the Humber - New Holland - added to the excitement. There were steam-hauled trains to convey ferry passengers almost from the water's edge on into the county of Lincoln. And there were green buses. Familiarity with United (in Scarborough and Whitby) and West Yorkshire (in York) - made much of the LRCC fleet recognisable, for many of the vehicles were standard Tilling Bristol/Eastern Coach Works products. But they were the *wrong colour*, thus intensifying the mystery and glamour. As the small boy became a teenager and then an adult, his sum of knowledge about the structure of bus companies in the United Kingdom broadened. The links between United, West Yorkshire and Lincolnshire, and why East Yorkshire and East Midland - and others briefly glimpsed such as Yorkshire Traction - were themselves apparently akin one to another, but not the same as the former trio, became clear and the mystery faded away like the morning mist, taking with it that peculiar aura of juvenile magic and glamour that surrounds youthful exploration and discovery.

It is fitting that Lincolnshire should so closely follow East Midland in this series of books. In 1942, when the constituents of British Electric Traction and Tilling went their separate ways, East Midland became a BET subsidiary whereas next-door neighbour Linconshire followed the Tilling path. Thus two adjacent companies, whose fleets had been broadly similar, began to take on the differing faces which became familiar to enthusiasts in the third quarter of the twentieth century.

The two companies started at around the same time in the late nineteen-twenties, too. East Midland rose out of the former W T Underwood operation; Lincolnshire was the Silver Queen Motor Omnibus Company Limited renamed. Silver Queen had originated in 1913. On 4th December of that year, Clacton & District Motor Services Limited had been registered. The Company's name was changed to Silver Queen Motor Omnibus Company Limited in July 1926. Lincolnshire started its programme of buying out competing operators as early as November 1928 when, jointly with East Midland and Trent, it took over Retford Motor Services Limited. A series of administrative changes of the late 1920s saw the LNER and LMSR become shareholders and in 1931 the routes of United Automobile Services Limited (ex-Underwood, ex-Progressive) in the Boston and Holbeach areas were transferred to Lincolnshire. In the two decades that followed, over fifty other operators were taken over, a programme which gave Lincolnshire depots and offices in many towns throughout the area.

The Tilling companies, including Road Car, came under the control of the British Transport Commission in 1948. Soon after that event, Road Car had 331 buses and coaches allocated to thirteen main depots, of which Lincoln with 79, Skegness with 48 and Grantham with 38 were the biggest; and nine outstations, including the writer's mysterious New Holland. At this time the fleet was covering twelve million miles annually and carrying thirty-eight million passengers.

A substantial acquisition in 1950 was that of the major operator Enterprise (Scunthorpe) Passenger Services Limited. This brought 150 vehicles and there were historical links with both United and East Midland. Two companies, named Enterprise and Silver Dawn respectively, were merged, in 1924, as Enterprise and Silver Dawn Motors Limited. The new company was acquired by W T Underwood, of Clowne, the following year and liquidated. It was reformed in 1927 to run the Scunthorpe and Frodingham branch of Underwood's successor, East Midland Motor Services Limited. Among its first vehicles had been four ADCs transferred from United. The Company's name was changed in 1947 and in 1950 it sold out to the British Transport Commission. Road Car, as the local incumbent, took on the routes, vehicles and premises.

The Transport Holding Company took over from the British Transport Commission in 1963 and on 1st January 1969 the newly created National Bus Company's commencing assets included Road Car. The remainder of the twentieth century has seen other important changes, and today Road Car is part of the Traction Group which also includes Yorkshire Traction, Strathtay Scottish Omnibuses Limited, Barnsley & District and Andrews of Sheffield.

THE FLEET

Restricted to a single word to describe the Road Car fleet, one could do a lot worse than choose "heterogeneous". The known fleet absorbed from Silver Queen in 1928 included the Chevrolet, Ford, Leyland, Reo and Wolseley marques. The same year saw the first new buses - five Tilling Stevens Motors with Beadle bodywork. The Retford Motor Services acquisition, also in 1928, brought a half-dozen Leyland PLSC Lions. A large number of small Chevrolets and a few more TSMs came new in 1929 and 1930. The name of the coachbuilder Rainforth comes into the story with some, or possibly all, of the Chevrolets. In the ensuing decade up to the outbreak of the Second World War, acquisitions of other operators brought examples of ADC, AEC, AJS, BAT, Bean, Bedford, Citroen, Commer, Crossley, Daimler, Dennis, Federal, Gilford, GMC, Guy, Morris, Overland, Star, Sunbeam, Thornycroft and Vulcan into the fleet.

Bodywork on many of the acquired buses remains unidentified, but coachbuilders' transfers inside various new and second-hand vehicles in the pre-war Road Car fleet included Applewhite, Bracebridge, Brush, Burlingham, Clark, Dennis, Duple, Eastern Counties, Eaton, Economy, Forbes Brebner, Harrington, Harrison, Hutson Brothers, Layne, Leyland, London Lorries, Rainforth, Strachan and Brown, Taylor, United, Weymann, Willowbrook and Wycombe. Yes, "heterogeneous" seems to fit the bill. Many of the second-hand vehicles were quickly withdrawn, in some cases without being repainted or even used.

The most significant groups of acquired vehicles came from United Automobile Services Limited on 1st January 1931 and Skegness Motor Services Limited on 27th November 1934. United contributed thirty-nine vehicles of AEC, Chevrolet, Guy,

Leyland, Triumph and Vulcan manufacture (the Triumph was an inspection motorcycle); and Skegness & District twenty-six, mainly Dennises but including some Vulcans, which were destined to be very long-lived in Road Car service.

In the same pre-war period, new purchases moved firmly over to Leyland, starting energetically in 1932 with an order for twenty Rainforth-bodied KP2 Cub 20-seaters. The first Tigers appeared in 1933, and for the rest of the decade Cubs and Tigers saw to new single-deck requirements. Double-deckers in the shape of TD1 and TD5 Titans came in 1931 and 1939. Then Road Car's plans, as were everyone else's, were disrupted by the war.

At the outbreak of war, LRCC had 306 vehicles in service, 158 of which were small buses with 20 or 24 seats. The trio of 1931 TD1s were the only double-deckers, joined soon after the declaration by a pair of TD5s.

The Company managed to pursue its policy of buying new Leylands early in the war, but then it had to take Bedford OWB 32-seaters in some strength. Double-deck fleet augmentation was painfully slow, despite the rapidly increasing need occasioned by the enormous upsurge of aerodrome building and Royal Air Force activity. Lincolnshire was not known as "Bomber County" for nothing, and Binbrook, Coningsby, Scampton and Waddington were but a few of the dozens of Royal Air Force stations requiring transport. Three Leyland TD7s and three Guy Arabs were all until 1944/5, when a handful of Bristol K6As arrived. Road Car must have been happy with the Bedfords and Bristols, for when hostilities were over further Bedfords (the post-war OB version) and Bristol K6As were ordered.

Second-hand acquisitions continued apace in the post-war period, including, in 1947, some AEC Regents and Leyland Titans, which were a minimum of fourteen years old, from Brighton Hove & District Omnibus Company Limited and Wigan Corporation respectively. New stock, apart from a few Leyland PD1A Titans and some Beadle chassisless single-deckers, followed the Bristol/Eastern Coach Works path, as befitted a state-owned operator.

The 150 vehicles acquired from Enterprise in 1950 were mainly AECs and Bedfords, with a sprinkling of Leylands and Guys and a solitary Daimler. 1950 was something of an *annus mirabilis* for Road Car, for it added a further 52 vehicles from three more acquired companies as well as over forty new vehicles.

That was virtually the end of the intake from acquired operators, but the 1950s saw a series of second-hand vehicles from other Tilling operators. Remarkably, some more Regents, by then two decades old, came from the Brighton operator in 1952. The following year a batch of ex-London Transport wartime Bristol K6As came, as did some Leyland TS7 Tigers from Crosville Motor Services, of Chester. In the remainder of the decade second-hand vehicles came from Tillings Transport, Southern Vectis, Hants and Dorset, Eastern Counties, West Yorkshire, Eastern National and Western National. Thus in comparison with, say, United, which had largely confined its second-hand vehicle intake to the pre-war period and had become highly standardised on new Bristol/ECW products by the early nineteen-fifties, Road Car remained a fascinating fleet of mixed provenance until much later. The last ex-London Transport double-decker, for example, lasted until 1960 and the last ex-Enterprise vehicle until 1961.

LRCC fleet numbers were originally alpha-numeric. The numbers ran in a single sequence, preceded by an appropriate letter or letters, "D" for Dennis, "G" for Gilford, "LC" for Leyland Cubs, "LT" for Tigers, etc., although the letters were gradually dropped. Few large operators escaped the need to renumber their fleets in the post-war period and Road Car was no exception. Its major renumbering was implemented in 1953 when a four-figure numerical series commencing at 1001 was introduced.

It is stressed that the pages of this album are neither a history nor a fleet list of the Lincolnshire Road Car Company Limited. They are rather a platform upon which to present the best of the Geoffrey Atkins Collection of photographs of the Company's vehicles across a period of sixty years. Readers seeking further information are referred to the PSV Circle's publication PE4 which covers the Lincolnshire Road Car Company from 1950 to 1979 and which incorporates Enterprise (Scunthorpe) Passenger Services Limited. PE4 is subtitled "LRCC Part Two"; Part One has not yet been published but is in preparation.

John Banks
Series Editor
Romiley, Chesire, January 2000

"ROAD CAR" IN THE LANDSCAPE -- In an evocative scene *(above)* at Bargate bus terminus, Boston in July 1936, Road Car vehicles blend into the canvas as if they had always been; yet the Company was less than a decade old. Leyland Tiger TS7 **LT395** (**FW6856**) was leaving for Skegness on service 57, one of the trunk routes taken over from United. Another Tiger, **LT403** (**FW6864**) was on the same service as far as Benington. These Tigers were a mere three months old, in sharp contrast to the 1929 Ford AA **FU9932** of Wright's Bus Service. Wright's business passed to Road Car in 1950. The old bus station in Lincoln *(below)* was a cramped affair but it had to suffice until palatial new premises were opened in 1959. Passengers were boarding AEC Regal **935** (**DFW78**), an ex-Enterprise vehicle, in the early 1950s.

SECOND-HAND AEC REGENTS

A fascinating group of pre-war, ex-Brighton, Hove & District AEC Regents joined the fleet in 1947 (2) and 1952 (3). **1907 (GW6271)**, one of the 1947 pair, was at Grantham bus station in February 1954 *(above)*. Its body was by Charles H. Roe and had replaced the original Tilling open-staircase unit in March 1949. Bristol LWL5G **2045 (HFW486)** of 1952 was alongside. From the 1952 trio, **1908 (GW6290)** is seen *(below)* at Richmond Drive, Skegness in July 1954. Also originally an open staircase bus, its Eastern Coach Works body had been fitted in 1944. Both Regents had been new in 1932 and were thus 22 years old when photographed.

EX-ENTERPRISE AEC REGALS

Above: Most Road Car AECs came from Enterprise in 1950. **1869** (**FFU856**) was a 1949 Willowbrook-bodied Regal III dual-purpose 35-seater which had been new less than a year before Enterprise sold out to the British Transport Commission. It was at Richmond Drive, Skegness in July 1954, on summer express service L from Scunthorpe. *Below:* In a June 1955 group at Waterside, Lincoln, ex-Enterprise **1853** (**EFW391**), a similar AEC Regal III, was alongside 1954 Bristol LD6G Lodekka **2301** (**KFW312**) and another ex-Enterprise vehicle, Guy Arab **1711** (**CFW1**). The Guy was a 1945 machine with a utility 55-seat lowbridge body by Roe.

BEADLE-LEYLAND CHASSISLESS BUSES -- *Above:* The integrally constructed bus - effectively a chassisless design - was by no means new in 1948. London Transport, for example, had placed a large batch of chassisless trolleybuses in service before the war. The machines constructed by the Dartford manufacturer John C. Beadle were innovative in that they used engines, gearboxes and running units from time-served conventional buses. **699 (EFU843)** was a Leyland-Beadle 33-seater. ***Below:*** From left to right we see Leyland-Beadle **716 (FFU968)**, Bedford-Beadle **722 (FFU157)**, Leyland Cub **520 (FW8873)**, Bedford OB **667 (DBE810)** with its striking rear-end design and, just visible alongside 667, 1925 Vulcan **343 (NR6648)**. Both photographs were at Grosvenor Road, Skegness in July 1949.

BEDFORD BUSES

Above: Road Car's sizeable fleet of wartime Bedford OWBs is represented by 1943's **622** (**CBE548**), whose Duple austerity bodywork seated 32. It was at Skegness Lawn motor park in July 1949.

Below: Photographed after the 1953 renumbering, **1120** (**DBE811**) was a 1947 Bedford OB with the same bizarre 30-seat bodywork by John C. Beadle of Dartford. The view dates from July 1956 and was taken in the old bus station in Grantham, from which the bus would trundle the eight miles down the A1 to Colsterworth.

DUPLE-BODIED BEDFORDS

Above: **936 (DFW90)** was another former Enterprise vehicle. It had been new in 1947 and was a Bedford OB with Duple 32-seat bodywork. It was photographed at Waterdale, Doncaster in June 1952.

Below: Among the more unusual Bedford OBs were the Skegness sea front machines. Two such vehicles, dating from 1949, were bought from Eastern National in 1958. They were fitted with 29-seat Duple coach bodies which were rebuilt as "twopence all the way" open-sided runabouts for seaside work. One wonders what supported the roof. **1003 (ONO89)** was at North Parade, Skegness in August 1959.

BEDFORD COACHES

Above: **1153** (**CTL460**), a 1948 example of the classic Bedford OB/Duple Vista combination, came from A. E. Olive, of Billinghay, in June 1950. It was originally numbered 32 by Road Car. In this July 1954 view it was at Drummond Road, Skegness.

Below: A world away in concept and style from the same chassis and coachbuilders. Bedford VAM14 45-seater **1601** (**EFE445E**) dated from 1967. It was at the Goose Fair at Nottingham Forest on private hire work. 1601 was one of a pair, withdrawn in 1974 and sold to the Southern Vectis Omnibus Company.

CHEVROLET AND DENNIS

Above: **C78** (**FW726**), seen here at the old bus station, Lincoln in July 1932 was a 1930 Chevrolet LQ fitted with Waveney 20-seat bodywork. Note the magnificent cast *Lincolnshire* name on the radiator top and the roof-mounted colour route light. LRCC did not display route numbers until 1935. In print, the ex-United numbers were shown in 1931, but no others. The colour lights were provided on all ordinary service buses until 1939.

Below: An agreement was made on 27th November 1934 for Lincolnshire to take over the business of Skegness Motor Service Limited. Twenty-six vehicles on Dennis, Reo and Vulcan chassis were transferred. The newest were a pair of 1934 Dennis Aces with Dennis Brothers coachwork. One was a bus and the other, **D339** (**FW5132**), had a 20-seat coach body complete with curtains and roof luggage rack. It was at Richmond Drive, Skegness in June 1939. The dappled roof was not an early attempt at anti-aircraft camouflage, it was simply the pattern of light and shade from nearby trees.

TILLING-STEVENS

Above: Rear angles of early coachwork are not common outside manufacturer's rather clinical official record views. This 31-seat, rear-entrance bus body by John C. Beadle, of Dartford, is seen at Grantham in May 1929. The chassis carrying it was a Tilling-Stevens B9 new to Lincolnshire in 1928. It is one of a pair, **TS12/13 (KP1988/89)**, though we do not know which.

Below: No doubt about the identity of this one: **TS79 (FW764)**, a Tilling-Stevens B10A with Beadle 32-seat bodywork, was photographed on private hire work not long after its 1930 arrival in the fleet. Both were clearly front-line vehicles when photographed, being labelled for trunk routes from Lincoln to Grantham (25 miles) and Skegness (42 miles), later numbered as 1 and 6. Note that the removable but rattling board on the older vehicle has been succeeded on TS79 by what we would now call "route branding". The land and buildings, which included the railway grain warehouse, behind TS79 later formed the site for Lincolnshire's new Lincoln bus station.

VULCANS -- **FU7327**, at Skegness station on a local service *(above)* in July 1929, was a 1927 VWBL model in the Skegness Motor Service Limited fleet. It had originally been owned by Tom Carey Limited and passed to LRCC in 1934 as No. 348. When compared with the LRCC Vulcan below it was a conventional 29-seat bus, though its two doors are noteworthy. It lasted into the early post-war years. **1022** (**NR7266**) *(below)* was a 1925 Skegness Motor Service Vulcan-bodied *char-à-bancs,* a type often miscalled "toastrack", on the Vulcan VSD chassis. LRCC acquired it as No. V344 in 1934 and had it rebuilt in 1946 with a Bedford engine and radiator, in which form it survived its 33rd birthday and was withdrawn in 1958. This classic sea-front runabout was at Sea View Road, Skegness in August 1958.

PRE-WAR LEYLAND TITANS

Above: Lincolnshire had few double-deckers at any time before the war. The impact of a trio of gleaming TD1 Titan 51-seaters in 1931 must have been considerable. **LT187 (FW2228)** was the first of them, seen here opposite the Pier, then the main departure point in Skegness for LRCC services, in May 1933. The through service over the 32 miles Skegness - Boston - Spalding was a combination of services 57 and 59, which had been similarly run by United as Nos. 53/52.

Below: Perhaps even more imposing in LRCC green were two Leyland-bodied TD5 56-seaters which came in 1939. **LT567 (AFU844)** was brand new in this June 1939 picture at Drummond Road, Skegness working the ex-United trunk route to Boston. These TD5s are believed to have been the last LRCC buses delivered with colour route lights.

LEYLAND TITANS AFTER THE WAR

Above: Wartime traffic conditions called for more double-deckers, a situation helped by a pair of Leyland-bodied 56-seat TD7 Titans in 1940. **1612 (BBE945)**, originally L1584, was at Newark's old bus station on a local service in August 1955, a year before its withdrawal. It was exported to Yugoslavia for further service. *Below:* Early post-war days were equally demanding of high-capacity buses. New Leyland Titans reappeared in 1948 with two PD1As carrying Eastern Coach Works lowbridge bodywork. This July 1949 Drummond Road, Skegness scene includes **691 (DFW568)**. The 42 miles on trunk service 6 to Lincoln would be memorable indeed.

LEYLAND LIONS

Above: Six PLSC1 Lions came to the fledgling LRCC from Retford Motor Services Limited in November 1928. This is **LL8 (RR8355)** in July 1929 at Skegness Parade. The bus was still in Retford's dark-red livery with fleet number 79 visible. This vehicle had Taylor 31-seat bodywork and lasted until 1950. The bus behind was identical and is believed to have been ex-Retford No. 80. *Below:* Ex-Retford Motor Services **6 (RR4402)** at Roman Bank, Skegness at 8.00 on a bright morning in June 1948. The Taylor bodywork, originally dual-doorway, was converted to front-entrance at an unknown date and was extensively rebuilt in 1946. The short coastal journeys were well-filled in the season.

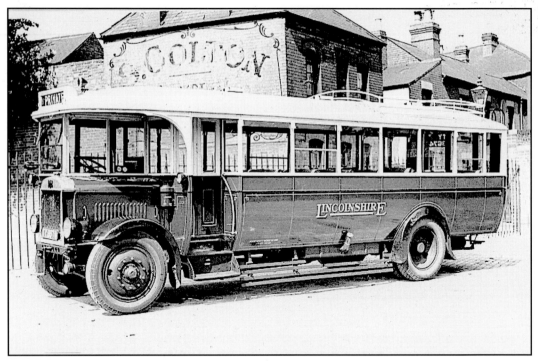

LEYLAND LIONS

Above: The massive injection of vehicles from United Automobile Services Limited on 1st January 1931 included seven PLSC3 Lions which United had acquired in 1928 from Amos, Proud & Company, of Choppington. One of them was Lincolnshire's **LL133 (TY3674)** which was photographed at Huntingdon Street, Nottingham in August 1933.

Below: One of two LT5A Lions with Leyland 35-seat, front-entrance bodies, taken into stock in 1934, was **LL274 (FW4489)**, seen here at the old bus station in Grantham in May 1935.

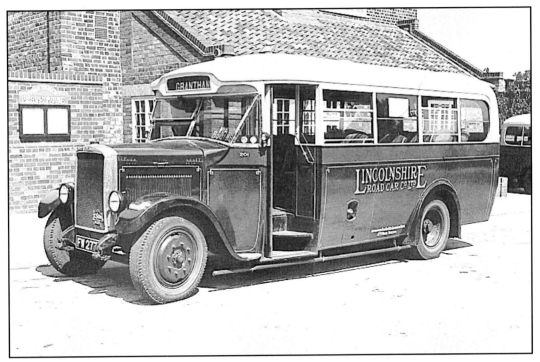

LEYLAND CUBS

Above: The coachbuilder Rainforth supplied 20-seat bodies for twenty KP2 Cubs in 1932. In August of the following year **201 (FW2779)** was at Grantham's old bus station. This was the longest-lived of the twenty. It survived into 1949 whereas the others all went between 1939 and 1947.

Below: For a batch of ten KP3 Cubs in 1934 Lincolnshire placed the bodywork order with Eastern Counties, of Lowestoft. They were 24-seaters. **LC266 (FW4481)** was brand new in this scene at Prince George Street bus station, Skegness. This batch of Cubs had also all gone by the end of 1949.

LEYLAND CUBS AND TIGERS

Above: For 1936's fifteen Cubs the model designation was KP201 and Brush supplied the 20-seat bodies. **LC418/19 (FW7091/2)** were together on relief duties at Roman Bank, Skegness in July 1936 having entered service the previous month. **Below:** The KP201/Brush combination continued in 1937 and 1938. One of 1938's batch, **LC534 (ABE341)** was on the Gainsborough service at Lincoln's old bus station in June 1938. It, too, was just one month old when photographed. **>> Opposite page: LT232 (FW3679)** was a 1933 TS4 Tiger with magnificent, canopied 30-seat coachwork by Rainforth. It was one of a pair which figured prominently in pre-war advertising literature. It was at Roman Bank, Skegness in June 1934.

LEYLAND TIGERS

Above: Roman Bank, Skegness was one of Geoffrey Atkins's favourite photography locations. He used it in June 1934 for this shot of 1933's **LT233 (FW3839)**, a Leyland-bodied 35-seat Tiger TS4 bus. *Below:* At 8.50 on a morning in July 1935 at Huntingdon Street, Nottingham **LT365 (FW5693)** was showing PRIVATE in the blind but was acting as a duplicate on the service to Mablethorpe. LT365 was a Brush-bodied TS7 Tiger with service-bus seating for 34. These Tigers appear to be the first buses in the fleet equipped to display a service number. The man pulling a handcart evokes a once common sight in city streets now - humanely - no more.

DUPLE-BODIED LEYLAND TIGERS

Above: Almost as flamboyant as the 1933 Rainforth-bodied 30-seaters were the 1935 centre-entrance Duple 31-seat coaches on TS7 Tiger chassis. There were four of them and we have two pictures of **LT376** (**FW5704**). In this view it was at Marine Drive, Scarborough in June 1935 with the driver watching the photographer from the comfort of the back seat. *Below:* The same coach at 8.45 on a bright August 1936 morning heading for Mablethorpe, seventy-seven miles away. Holiday suitcases can be seen in the roof-mounted luggage-rack. Another of the batch is the third vehicle in this Huntingdon Street, Nottingham queue of four.

LEYLAND TIGERS -- *This page:* **LT372** (**FW5700**) and **LT403** (**FW6864**), Brush- and Leyland-bodied TS7 Tigers, show clearly the pre-war livery of dark- and light-green with off-white window pillars and roof. The photographs were at Huntingdon Street, Nottingham in July 1935 *(above)* and twelve months later at Drummond Road, Skegness *(below)*. As with the similar Tiger on page three, the Company had not yet allocated the service numbers for the coastal routes north of Skegness, and had left a white square on the blinds to be filled in later. LT372 and LT403 dated respectively from 1935 and 1936. **>> Opposite page:** The following year's TS7s with Brush 34-seat bodies are epitomised in this splendid portrait of **LT477** (**FW8830**) at Huntingdon Street, Nottingham in August 1937.

HAZARDS AND RESTRICTIONS -- *Above:* At Roman Bank, Skegness in June 1939. **LT404 (FW6865)**, a 1936 Leyland-bodied TS7, splashes its way towards Ingoldmells on service 93. *Below:* By May 1940 the war had produced khaki roofs, white wing-tips and guard rails and headlamp masks for 1937's TS7 Tiger **LT481 (FW8834)** and 1936's KP201 Cub **LC411 (FW7084)** at the old bus station in Newark where LT481 has just arrived from Sleaford on the 35. **>> *Opposite page:*** Also in wartime dress in Newark early in the conflict was **LT586 (BFU225)**, a one-off "Leyland Light Six", or "Lion Six". It was described variously as an LT6 and an LS1 in Leyland records. "Private" and "Relief Car" would not have revealed much to an invading enemy: might, indeed, have caused confusion as maps were vainly searched.

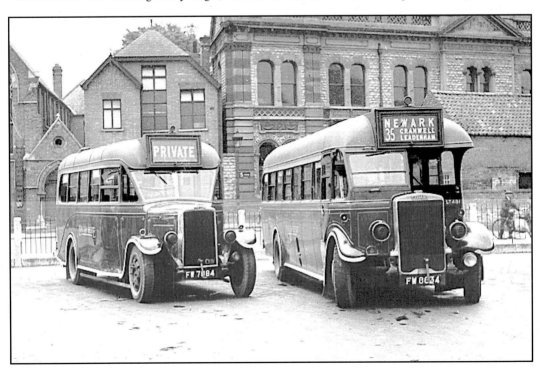

LEYLAND TIGERS IN THE POST-WAR PERIOD

Above: **1483 (BBE770)**, new in April 1940 as LT573, was a Weymann-bodied 34-seat TS8 Tiger, seen in July 1956 at the old bus station, Grantham waiting to leave on the 34B for Sleaford. The colour route light and pre-war livery were long since gone.

Below: **1413 (FW5700)** as rebodied in March 1950 by Burlingham. The same vehicle with its original body is illustrated on page 28 *(upper)*. This May 1956 view was at the old bus station, Lincoln from which 1413 would take the secondary roads over the rolling wolds to Sleaford.

>> *Opposite page:* At Drummond Road, Skegness in July 1949 three body types were spotted side-by-side. From left to right: 1939's **560 (AFU837)** was a 34-seater by Weymann, 1936's **395 (FW6856)** was a Burlingham post-war rebody and 1937's **485 (FW8838)** had a Brush 34-seat body.

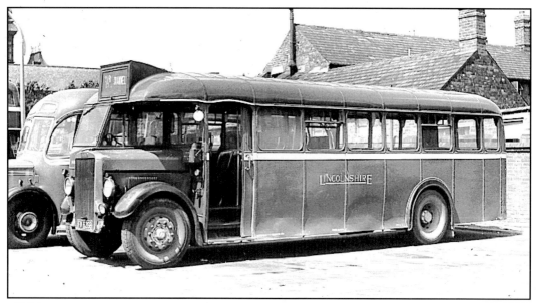

REBUILT LEYLAND TIGERS AND NEW BRISTOLS

This page: A phenomenon of the wartime period was the rebuilding of pre-war bodywork in an attempt to keep buses and coaches serviceable for a few more years at a time of new vehicle shortage. **1401** **(FW6268)** *(above)*, seen at Grantham in 1955, was a 1935 TS7 Tiger whose Leyland body was overhauled by Eastern Coach Works at Irthlingborough in 1943. 1938's TS8 Tiger **531** **(ABE338)** *(below)* had a Harrington body which was similarly overhauled in 1944. It was in Nottingham in 1950.

>> Opposite page: Bristol chassis entered the fleet in ever increasing numbers for all types of duty after 1948. **738** **(FFW192)**, a 1949 L6A with Eastern Coach Works dual-purpose 31-seat body, was in Nottingham in August 1950. Lincolnshire's design of destination box makes a small but significant difference to the appearance of this otherwise typical Tilling Group vehicle.

BRISTOL SINGLE-DECKERS

Above: **2009** (**FFW194**) was another of the 1949 L6A dual-purpose 31-seaters. When seen at Nottingham in May 1957 its livery was in effect the service bus scheme plus a cream flash. The full array of opening windows was distinctive. *Below:* The photographer spotted and promptly recorded a rebuilt destination screen box on Bristol L6B **2003** (**DFW359**) at Nottingham in July 1957. 2003 was a 1947 delivery, originally numbered 687. It was another dual-purpose machine, thought to have been a 33-seater in later life, although delivered with the standard 31 seats for this style of Eastern Coach Works body. The last bay housed a by then disused destination screen.

LONGER BRISTOL SERVICE BUSES

Above: Even though the clock in the background reads 8.40am, this was the 8.30 departure from Huntingdon Street, Nottingham to Mablethorpe one fine day in May 1951. **793 (GFW854)** was a 1951 LL6B which, with the Bristol six-cylinder engine, would have been more than capable of making up the lost time, though it was not an easy road after Lincoln. *Below:* LWL5G **2040 (HBE757)**, on the other hand, would have been very sluggish with only five-cylinder Gardner power to haul a 30ft x 8ft 39-seater around. It was at Grantham in June 1954, ready to work the fourteen-mile rambling rural service eastwards to Billingborough.

EARLY BRISTOL CHASSIS

<< *Opposite page:* In this June 1955 view the Nottingham to Mablethorpe run was being entrusted to a second-hand 1939 Bristol L5G. **2077** (**CVF883**) was one of a batch of seventeen bought from the Eastern Counties Omnibus Company Limited in 1954. All had Eastern Coach Works bodies: nine 35-seat buses and eight, including 2077, dual-purpose 32-seaters. A late departure with this vehicle would have been a more serious matter.

Above: As the war ground on Lincolnshire found itself with the same shortage of serviceable vehicles that afflicted most other operators. The problem was alleviated by the intake of 32-seat Bedford OWBs in some quantity, but double-deckers were few and far between in the war years just when they were becoming more necessary. There had been a Leyland Titan TD7 and three Guy Arabs in 1942, then in 1944/5 five Bristol K6As with Park Royal austerity 56-seat bodywork were allocated to LRCC by the Ministry of Supply. These had chassis numbers in Bristol's build sanction "W1" and were typical of the era in lacking alloys in their manufacture. They were thus rather heavy. The bodywork, too, was built with basic materials to an angular design decreed by the Ministry, which forbade any attempt at rounding or smoothing the contours. Slatted wooden seats were often provided although these were usually replaced in the post-war years.

The first of Lincolnshire's quintet was **649** (**CFU506**), seen here at Grantham's old bus station in November 1951 while working on service to Sleaford.

BRISTOL DOUBLE-DECKERS

Above: Nottingham to Grantham by ex-London Transport Bristol. When London disposed of its utility Bristols in the early 1950s they were eagerly snapped up by Tilling Group operators. Lincolnshire acquired seven Duple-bodied K6As in 1953, including **2107** (**HGC236**), seen at Huntingdon Street, Nottingham in October 1954. Although these K6As were regarded as "wartime" buses, they were built after the war had ended. *Below:* Night photography was a Geoffrey Atkins speciality. 1947's K6A **683** (**DFW355**) was also on the twenty-four-mile Nottingham to Grantham service, this time in April 1948. The postwar Tilling destination display appears at its brilliant best.

BRISTOL DOUBLE-DECKERS -- *Above:* 662 (DBE188) was a very early postwar K6A chassis. Its chassis number was in the same "W3" build sanction as the ex-London Transport vehicles, although it did not enter service until July 1946. In this view it was at St Mark's Street, Lincoln in the following August. The bus was displaying an ineffective "1D" route number for its local journey. Despite Lincolnshire's reputation as a flat county, this route involved a severe climb up Station Road into Waddington.

Below: **756 (GBE843)** was a 1950 K5G. The side windows were now to the postwar ECW standard, whereas on 662 above they had been to a semi-austerity style. Nevertheless, 756 had reverted to Lincolnshire's own style of destination box. It was at the old bus station in Grantham in July 1952.

BRISTOL DOUBLE-DECKERS -- *Above:* Another of the 1950 K5Gs, **2134 (GBE844)**, was modified in the late 1950s by the fitment of a Cave-Brown-Cave heating system and a revised front panel which incorporated a Bristol Lodekka grille. It ran thus until withdrawal in 1965. In this picture it was at Grantham in March 1962. ***Below:*** **778 (GFW279)** was a 1951 KS6B with four-bay (instead of five) ECW bodywork, seen arriving in Lincoln on the long run from Skegness. Across the road in this August 1951 St Mark's Street view is the rare sight of the offside-rear of an ex-Thomas Tilling and Brighton, Hove & District AEC Regent. **657 (GN6214)** dated from 1931. Its Brush body was fitted in 1946 before the vehicle was put into service by LRCC later that year.

TO THE SEASIDE BY BUS

The photographer recorded this view of Linconshire's 1948 Bristol K6B because of the non-standard, larger destination screen, an interesting cross between the Tilling pattern and Linconshire's own. Sixteen-year-old **2125 (FBE323)** was in immaculate condition in this September 1964 view taken shortly before it was withdrawn from service later that year. The photograph was taken at Drummond Street, Skegness.

WINTRY WEATHER

Above: A misty morning at Huntingdon Street, Nottingham in February 1953 and Lincolnshire's one-month-old Bristol KSW6G **972** (**JBE871**) was on the trunk service 33C to Grantham. The 60-seat Eastern Coach Works body was fitted with platform doors. *Below:* Snow was on the ground twenty-four miles away at Grantham in March 1955 when **2143** (**KBE181**) was spotted in the old bus station at the other end of the same 33C service. The bus was another 1953 KSW6G with platform doors, originally fleet number 990 in the earlier numbering scheme. The Tilling three-part destination display has finally supplanted the Lincolnshire "special".

LONGER AND WIDER COACHES

The 30ft-long fully fronted ECW coach body which appeared on Bristol LL (7ft 6ins) and LWL (8ft) chassis in the early 1950s quickly attracted the soubriquet "Queen Mary". Lincolnshire had a batch of ten, four on LL6B and six on the wider LWL6B chassis. They were all front-entrance 35-seaters and we illustrate two of the LWLs. **955** (**HBE509**) *(above)* was delivered in June 1951, **958** (**HBE512**) a month earlier. Both were at Huntingdon Street, Nottingham, in May 1952 and September 1951 respectively. 1951's deliveries included examples of KS6B, LL5G, LL6B, LWL5G and LWL6B Bristols as well as two rebuilt and rebodied AEC Regals.

THE BRISTOL SC

The four-cylinder-engined Bristol SC4LK Eastern Coach Works-bodied 35-seater was an attempt at providing a smaller, lighter bus for sparsely trafficked rural routes; it was perhaps the "midibus" of the 1950s in an era when such marketing expressions had not the vogue they have today. The SC was not as common as some other varieties of Bristol at that time; such fleets as United, West Yorkshire, Bristol and the whole of the Scottish Bus Group had none. Lincolnshire built up a considerable fleet of SCs in the second half of the 'fifties and up to 1961, including **2468 (NFE439)** *(above)* and **2482 (OVL491)**. They were at Grantham in April 1962 and Broad Marsh, Nottingham on an unspecified date.

BRISTOL SC COACHES -- Above: The SC as a coach, or "dual-purpose", 33-seater was even rarer, and again Lincolnshire was one of the places to see them. Road Car took a batch of ten in 1957 and a further five the following year. The bodyshell was very similar to that provided for the service-bus version; the biggest difference was in the ornamental grille, and the livery was reversed. **2602 (OFW800)**, one of the 1957 machines, was at Huntingdon Street, Nottingham on service A to Mablethorpe in August 1958. **Below:** The dual-purpose SCs were altered to 35-seat service bus specification in the late 1960s and early 1970s, as demonstrated by **2606 (OFW803)**, seen at the old bus station in Grantham in April 1974. Service 20 to Spalding was ex-United but had disappeared entirely by 1984.

THE BRISTOL LS

The 45-seat ECW "light saloon" on the Bristol LS chassis, revolutionised Tilling fleets in the 1950s. It was responsible for the consignment of vast numbers of traditional, forward-engined Bristol L 35-seaters to an early demise, when their only offence had been that of being too small. It has been claimed that the L could not be used as a one-man bus, but several companies successfully converted the type for just such use. The service-bus version of the LS usually had five-cylinder Gardner power, which made the type rather sluggish and difficult to keep to time. 1952's **978** (**JFU294**) *(above)* was at Newark in June 1953 and 1956's coach-seated **2218** (**MFU412**) at Nottingham in July 1956, bound for Butlin's at Skegness.

BRISTOL LS COACHES

The LS also appeared in "dual-purpose" form in many fleets, usually with 41 comfortable, high-backed seats. Lincolnshire's 1955 - 1957 examples were perhaps slightly less usual in retaining five-cylinder engines despite their intended use on express work. Lincolnshire had earlier bought some fully fledged coaches on the LS chassis with six-cylinder engines, but clearly had fuel economy in mind for the "dual-purpose" machines. Expert opinion today is not automatically in agreement that the 5HLW engine *was* more economical, as it had to be driven very hard for much of the time to compensate for its lack of power. 1955's **2212** (**MFU406**) *(above)* and *1956's* **2223** (**OFU434**) were both on express work, to Mablethorpe and Cleethorpes respectively, at Nottingham in May 1955 and Peterborough in June 1957. The body shell included bus-style destination boxes, and the only structural concession to "express" status was the winged "Bristol - ECW" emblem on the front.

BRISTOL LS COACHES

Above: In an unusual half-and-half livery, LS5G 41-seater **3010 (PBE212)** was at Huntingdon Street, Nottingham in June 1959. 3010 had been 2228 when new in 1957 and was again renumbered, as 2660, in 1962. It was reseated to 43 in 1968.

Below: **2262 (NFW543)** was a 39-seat coach on the LS6G chassis. It had been new in April 1956 and was renumbered 2812 in 1958 and again to 2012 in 1968. In this view it was at the same place two years earlier, but was not so badly hemmed in by parked carts as the left-hand coach above.

BRISTOL LS COACHES

Above: A number of detail improvements around the front panel and windscreen area combined to make the 1956 style of ECW 39-seat coach body on the LS chassis *(see page 50, lower)* rather different from the earlier version, typified by **974 (JFU290)** which was new in September 1952. The vehicle was at Canal Street, Nottingham in May 1953. *Below:* Another of the 1956 LS6Gs, **NFW541**, was rebuilt as a dual-purpose 39-seater in January 1968. Originally No. 2260, then **2810**, the vehicle was at Newark in July 1970. The mixed-size lettering on the destination blind indicates a short working on service 35 to Brant Broughton.

THE BRISTOL MW -- Above: 1961's **2812** (**RFE461**) was an MW6G 39-seater to full coach specification including inward-opening slam door. It was six months old when seen at Huntingdon Street, Nottingham in September 1961. *Below:* **2076** (**RFE471**) had the smaller five-cylinder Gardner engine for its duties as a dual-purpose 41-seater. Originally 3026, then 2676, it was renumbered 2076 and given bus seats and a revised livery in 1971. In September of that year it was photographed at Newark. In the widespread reduction from three- to two-part destination displays, Lincolnshire adopted the T-style for several years. **>>** *Opposite page:* 2233 (**NVL158**), dating from July 1958 and photographed at Newark in September 1963, had 43 more comfortable seats. The T-style screen is again in evidence.

EARLY BRISTOL LODEKKAS

Above: Among Lincolnshire's first Lodekkas in 1954 was **2308** (**KFW319**), an LD6G 58-seater fitted with platform doors. This bright, wintry, March 1955 day found it leaving Grantham for Lincoln.

Below: LD6B Lodekka **2319** (**LFW327**) came the following year and was also six-cylinder powered, but with a Bristol rather than a Gardner unit. It entered service in April 1955 and was photographed at Richmond Drive, Skegness the following August. It was working on local service 93 between the railway station and Butlin's holiday camp.

MORE LODEKKAS

Above: Another of the 1954 LD6Bs, **2309** (**LFW317**), shown after repaint into a reversed livery for seaside duties at Skegness as a successor to the Vulcan runabouts. It was at the Pier in August 1967.

Below: **2328** (**NBE131**), another of the 1955 delivery of Bristol-engined LDs, was working the Grantham town service in August 1956. The scene at the old bus station includes a magnificent Humber Super Snipe taxi, redolent of the era when enormous limousine versions of contemporary private cars were put to such use, bringing much character to cab ranks and station forecourts.

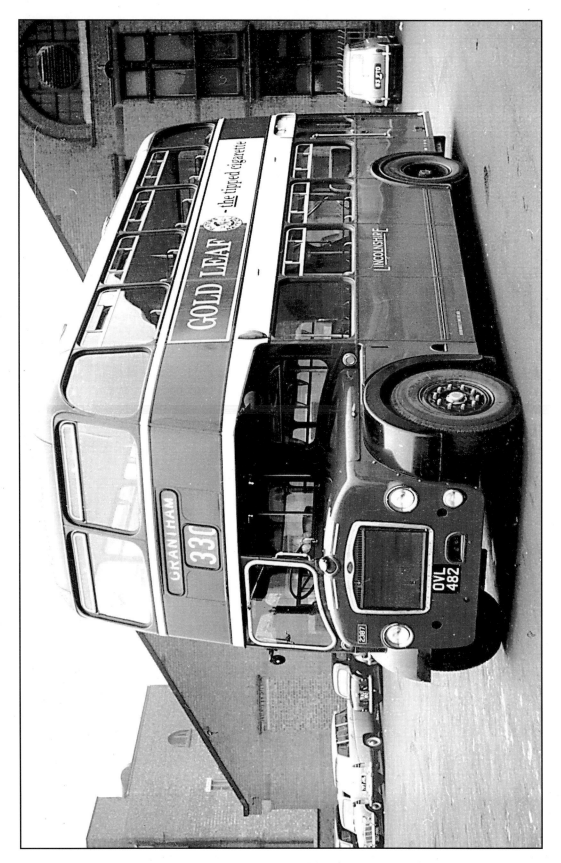

THE BRISTOL FS LODEKKA

<< *Opposite page:* A fine portrait of **2387** (**OVL482**), a 1961 Bristol FS5G. When this January 1962 picture was taken the bus, still in shiny, new condition, had been in service for over six months and had worked through its first winter.

This page: The concept of five-cylinder engines for double-deckers was pursued more by Road Car than most other Tilling operators because of its generally flat operating territory. This example of the FS5G, **2515** (**VFE964**), was an April 1964 delivery, photographed at Skegness and Newark in 1964 and 1970.

LONGER LODEKKAS and MAXIMUM CAPACITY SINGLE-DECKERS

Above: The rear-entrance, 30-ft.-long FL Lodekka was a rare bird. Road Car had a batch of five delivered in December 1960 and January 1961 of which **2704** (**OVL488**) was the last. It was caught, in a shot which stresses the length of this Lodekka/ECW variation, leaving Richmond Drive, Skegness for Ingoldmells in August 1970. *Below:* Much more common than the FL was the forward-entrance FLF. This one, **2508** (**TVL309**), was an FLF6G, in its first month of service in July 1962, at St Mark Street, Lincoln, setting off for Waddington R.A.F. Camp on service 1D.

>> *Opposite page:* **1203** (**AFE473B**), a 1964 Bristol RELL6G 54-seater, at Grantham in March 1970.

DEVELOPMENT OF THE BRISTOL RE

Above: The Bristol RE was produced in a version with a higher chassis frame, known as the RELH, for bodywork to coach specification. Lincolnshire's first of this variation on a theme was delivered in December 1964 as fleet number **1401** (**VVL730**), which Geoffrey Atkins photographed at Nottingham Broad Marsh in April 1969. *Below:* Later RELL6G service buses had a revised, flat-front design surmounted by a peaked roof. **1213** (**JVL359G**), seen at Grantham in April 1982, had been a July 1969 purchase. The drab all-over green and the general unkempt appearance typified the sorry state of many fleets in NBC days.

NATIONAL BUS COMPANY ERA BRISTOLS

Above: **1210** (**KFE635H**) entered service in December 1969, almost a year after the NBC began its existence on 1st January of that year. It had 44 seats and two doors. The provision of a central exit resulted in the loss of nine seats over the contemporary single-door version of the same vehicle and was not always felt to be an advantage once the novelty had worn off. The writer recalls travelling on a similar vehicle quite soon after it had entered service and being surprised to see both crew and passengers totally ignoring the centre exit, whose stairwell was used as an extra area for standing passengers.

Below: The most eagerly awaited new bus for decades was perhaps the Bristol VR. Originally a 36-ft. chassis with longitudinally mounted engine in the offside rear corner, the type soon settled down as a 30-footer with transversely mounted rear engine. LRCC's **1904** (**JVL619H**) was carrying the "East Notts" fleetname when photographed at Newark bus station in October 1985. 1904 had been new in August 1969. The 403 service number demonstrates the widespread regional groupings of new three-figure route identification in the National Bus Company era. An organised, logical system was thought to be more important than the underestimated virtues of stability and continuity.

THE BRISTOL LH

Above: The Bristol LH was the standard small single-decker in many NBC fleets. Service bus bodywork was usually specified but some operators saw a potential for coaching or "dual-purpose" use. Lincolnshire took some LHs in 1970 of which six were dual-purpose 41-seaters. **1665 (KVL451H)** was at Nottingham Broad Marsh in August 1970 when about three months old. *Below:* Three LRCC Bristol LHs at Newark bus station in August 1975. **1010 (RFE432K)** and **1035 (WFE839M)** were 43-seat service buses with Perkins and Leyland engines respectively, dating from 1972 and 1974; **1954 (GVL910F)**, on the right of the trio, was a very early, 1968, example of the type, with Perkins engine and dual-purpose seating for 41.

DEDICATED LHs

Above: Route branding, or "town branding", is a relatively new phenomenon. Lincolnshire had a network of rural routes known as "Country Courier" in use in the mid-1980s. Its special livery was applied to Bristol LH6L **1042 (LTL661P)** which had been new in November 1975. It was at Newark in May 1984, working the two 437 journeys which rambled down country lanes every Wednesday.

Below: Another LH6L, a 1978 purchase numbered **1065 (DTL541T)**, was repainted as "The Newton Rider" at Grantham, with the apple helpfully reminding us of Sir Isaac Newton's birth in the town. In December 1987 it was handily placed for its elaborate livery to be captured on film by Geoffrey Atkins as it set off on a local journey.

>> Overleaf: SIXTY YEARS CELEBRATED -- The Lincolnshire Road Car Company celebrated its first sixty years in 1988 by repainting a Bristol VR in an appropriate livery. The bus had two fleetnames, that of 1928 on the left and from 1988 on the right. The inset pictures show us how the Leyland coach design developed in the LRCC fleet across almost the same span of years. The Tiger TS7 with Brush coachwork, **LT363 (FW5691)**, dated from 1935 while the 47-seat ECW-bodied Leyland Leopard PSU3G/4RT, **1458 (AVL747X)**, was a 1982 purchase. 1458 was the last Leopard bought new by Road Car and was converted to a dual-purpose 53-seater in April 1992. It was photographed in Skegness in July 1988.